How Many Carmens?

by Lucy Floyd
illustrated by T. L. Ary

Harcourt

Orlando   Boston   Dallas   Chicago   San Diego

Visit *The Learning Site!*

www.harcourtschool.com

How can you measure something?
You can use crayons, spoons,
bottles, or straws! You can measure
with lots of different things!

You can use beans for measuring. This truck is ten beans long.

Blocks can be used, too. The dollhouse is 15 blocks high.

What do you like to eat for a treat?
You can use your treats to measure
things!

How many apples high is the hat?

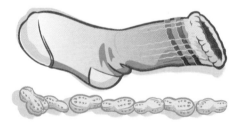

How many peanuts long is the
sock?

Do you like to snuggle up with a stuffed animal? You can use your animals to measure!

How many cats high is the plant? How many dogs long is the pillow?

Take a minute and look around you. What would you like to measure? What could you use to measure it?

There is one thing you can always use—yourself!

Carmen is using her hands to measure the fish tank. It is six hands high!

Now Carmen measures the quilt with her hands.

How many hands long is the quilt?

How many hands long is the game?

Carmen measures the paper snake with her arm. It's about one arm long.

She thinks that the jump rope is about four arms long. What do you think?

Carmen uses her feet, too. She has on sneakers so she measures the rug in sneakers.

How many sneakers long is the rug?

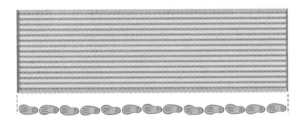

How many sneakers long is the mat?

Now Carmen wants to use her whole body to measure things. The screen is taller than Carmen.

Carmen thinks that the bench is about one Carmen long. What do you think?

How many Carmens high is the lamp?

You can measure the same way Carmen is measuring. Use yourself to measure things around you!

Now Carmen is going to do her homework. She makes a tool for measuring. She needs things the same size, so she uses paper clips.

Carmen starts by writing what she will do. She draws each step.

Here is the chart Carmen makes.

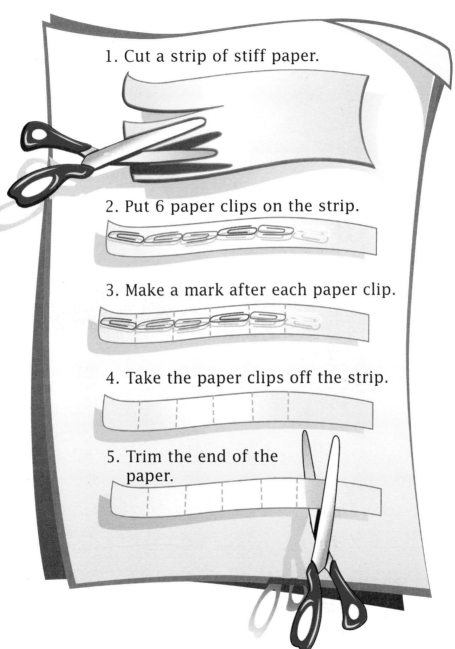

1. Cut a strip of stiff paper.

2. Put 6 paper clips on the strip.

3. Make a mark after each paper clip.

4. Take the paper clips off the strip.

5. Trim the end of the paper.

Carmen makes a ruler to use for measuring. She calls each box on the ruler a "clip." There are six clips in all.

Carmen's Clip Ruler

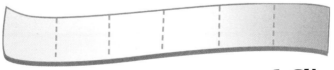

1 Clip

Carmen uses her ruler to measure small things. The bag is six clips high.

How many clips long is the nut?

How many clips high is the glass?

How many clips long is the clock?

Now make your own ruler! You can use Carmen's chart on page 13. If you wish, think of another way to make a ruler.

Use your ruler to measure the things on this page. Then measure things all around you!